Check out all of the books in the Tell Me About Dinosaurs Series

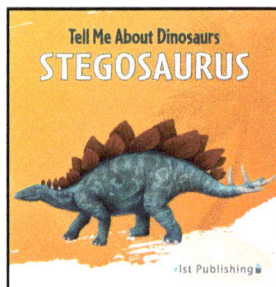

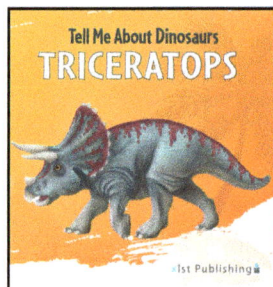

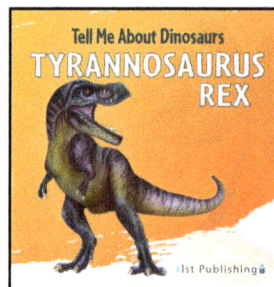

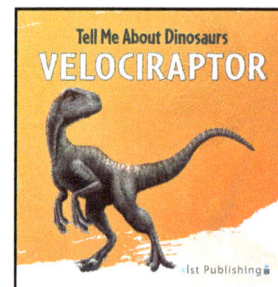

Tell Me About Dinosaurs
ANKYLOSAURUS
Xist Publishing

Tell Me About Dinosaurs
BRACHIOSAURUS
Xist Publishing

Tell Me About Dinosaurs
SPINOSAURUS
Xist Publishing

Tell Me About Dinosaurs
STEGOSAURUS
Xist Publishing

Tell Me About Dinosaurs
TRICERATOPS
Xist Publishing

Tell Me About Dinosaurs
TYRANNOSAURUS REX
Xist Publishing

Tell Me About Dinosaurs
VELOCIRAPTOR
Xist Publishing

Published in the United States by Xist Publishing
www.xistpublishing.com
© 2025 Copyright Xist Publishing

First Edition
Hardcover ISBN: 978-1-5324-5515-5
Paperback ISBN: 978-1-5324-5516-2
eISBN: 978-1-5324-5514-8

PUBLISHED IN TEXAS

Tell Me About Dinosaurs
ANKYLOSAURUS

Marjorie Seevers

xist Publishing

6 feet tall

30 feet long

Ankylosaurus was a heavy dinosaur.

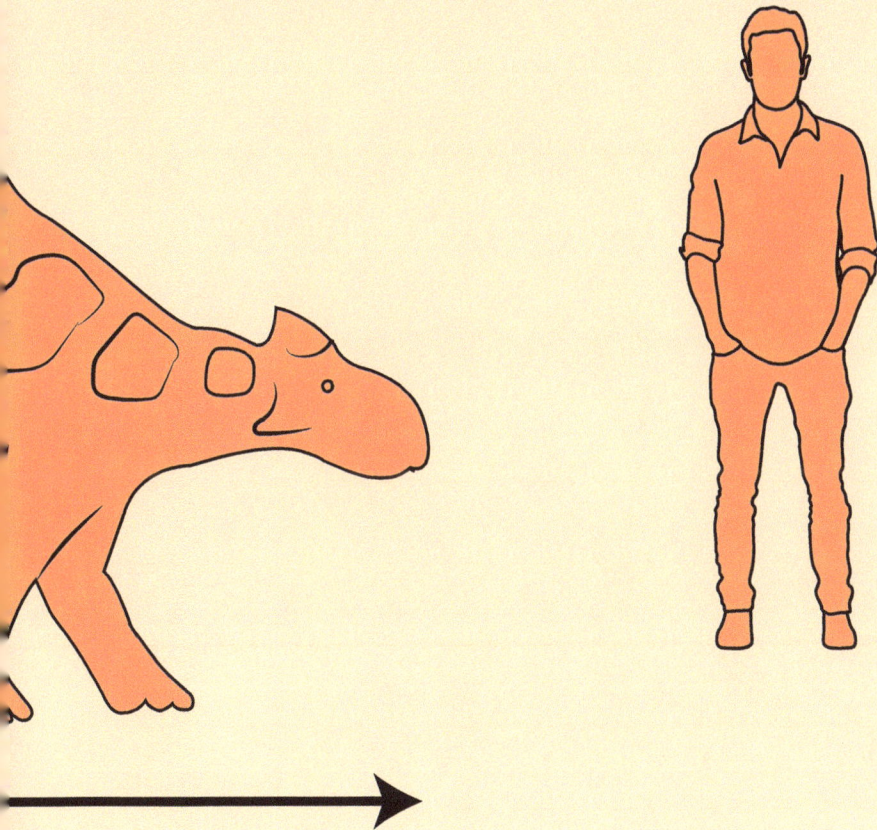

It ate plants.

Ankylosaurus had a thick, armored body.

It had a large club on its tail.

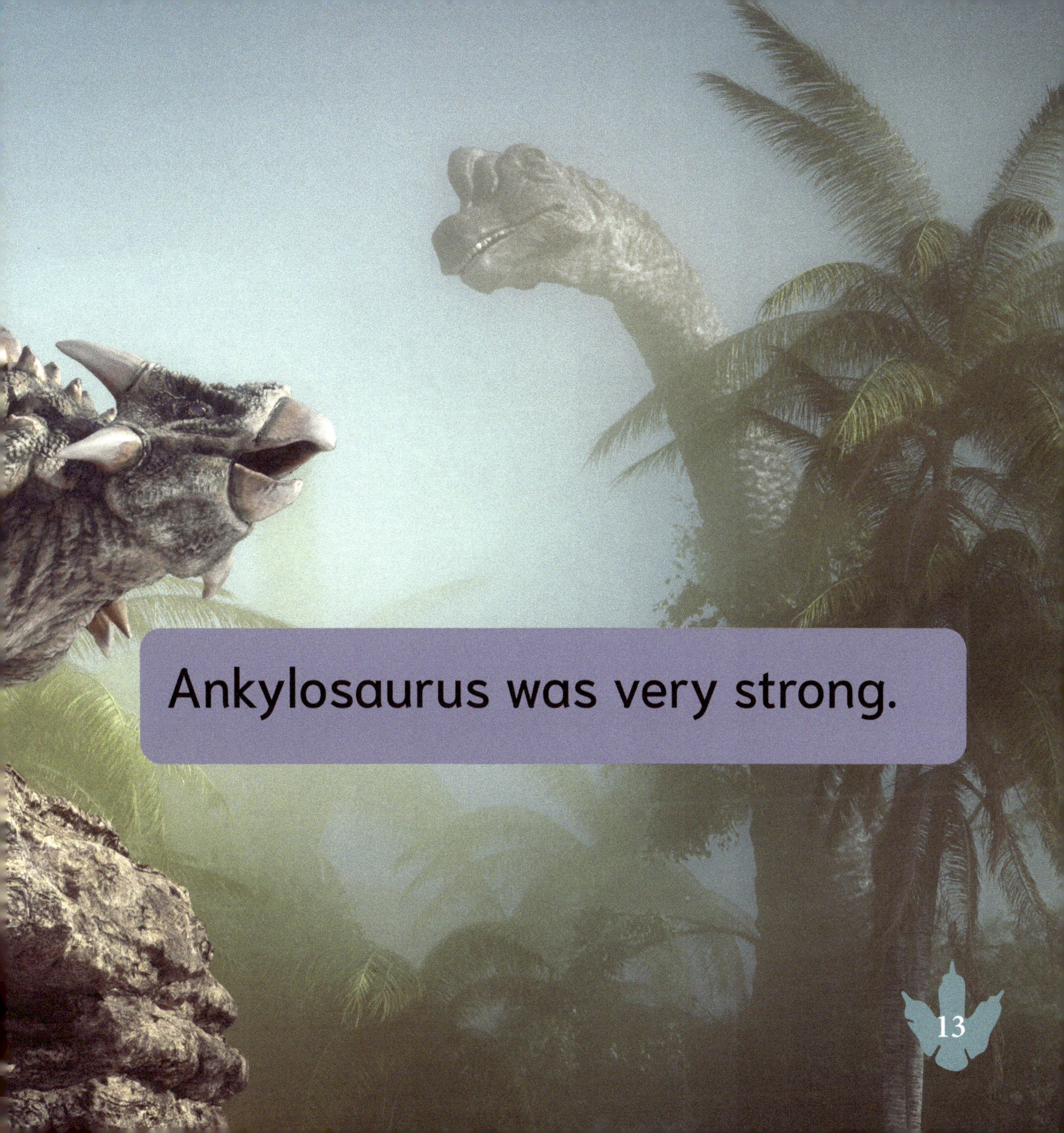

Ankylosaurus was very strong.

Its armor helped protect it from predators.

Ankylosaurus bones are called fossils.

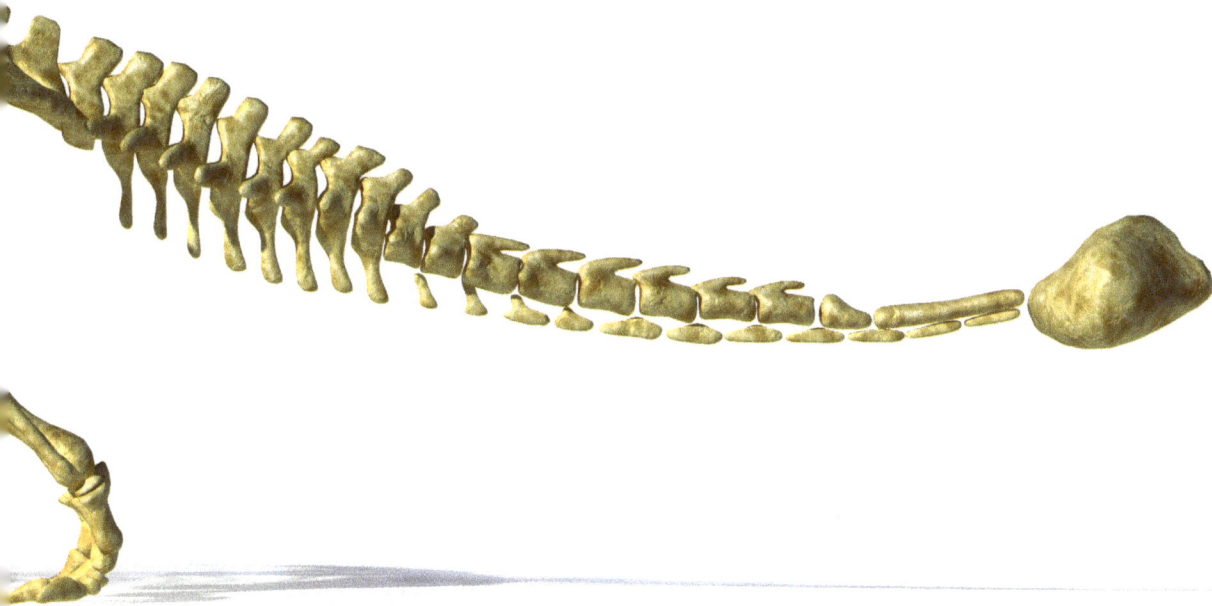

Which dinosaur is an Ankylosaurus?

What did Ankylosaurus eat?

www.ingramcontent.com/pod-product-compliance
Lightning Source LLC
LaVergne TN
LVHW070835080426
835508LV00031B/3480